The Stoic Science of Happiness

Aligning Ancient Philosophy with Positive Psychology

Table of Contents

Chapter 1. Introduction

In this enlightening Special Report, we delve into an enriching exploration of "The Stoic Science of Happiness: Aligning Ancient Philosophy with Positive Psychology". With a dash of joyous insight and a touch of sagacious understanding, traverse a thought-provoking journey that harmoniously unites the ancient wisdom of Stoicism with the vibrant field of Positive Psychology. From Seneca's tranquil tranquility to Seligman's flourishing individuals, we invite you to unearth an enthralling pathway towards authentic contentment, unraveling how these two fascinating domains intersect, influencing our pursuit to greater well-being. Let's embark together on this lively voyage, where antiquity embraces modernity, guiding you to embrace life with resilience, equanimity, and enduring happiness. Promptly purchase this Special Report and allow yourself to be irresistibly drawn into a remarkable discourse that whispers timeless wisdom and resonates with contemporary science.

Chapter 2. Stoicism Defined: A Primer

Stoicism, an intellectual tradition of philosophy probed in this context, is much more than a simple presentation of principles. Its roots spread wide across centuries, anchored firmly in the fertile soils of ancient Greece and Rome. Let's begin our exploration by uncovering the fundamental concepts and notions that provide the framework of Stoicism.

2.1. Stoicism: The Birth and Growth

Originating in the Hellenistic period, around the third century BC, Stoicism was founded by Zeno of Citium. Zeno, a merchant turned philosopher after a shipwreck, sought answers in Athens, the intellectual powerhouse of the ancient world. Studying under the Cynic Crates, the seeds of Stoicism were first planted. These seeds would grow to become one of the most influential philosophical movements of western thought.

Furthermore, three towering figures whose ideas blossomed during the Roman Empire were instrumental in propagating the tenets of Stoicism: Seneca, Epictetus, and the emperor Marcus Aurelius. Their treatises, letters, and meditations offer an enriching glimpse into the living practice of Stoicism.

2.2. Stoic Philosophy: The Cardinal Virtues

Central to Stoic philosophy is the idea of 'virtue being the sole good'. Stoicism proposes that a virtuous life is a good life. However, to truly grasp Stoicism, we must understand the four fundamental virtues it recognizes: wisdom, courage, justice, and temperance. Stoics believe that cultivating these virtues leads to a life of equanimity and fulfillment.

Wisdom, the master virtue, is broadly conceived as the knowledge of what is good, indifferent, and bad. Wisdom is the ability to navigate life using reason, which Stoics deem as the defining attribute of humans.

Courage refers not only to physical bravery but also to the moral courage to defend what is right, even in the face of adversity.

Justice, the third virtue, pertains to fair dealings with others. Stoicism encourages us to acknowledge our social nature and treat fellow beings with kindness and respect.

Finally, temperance is the virtue of self-restraint, maintaining balance and moderation in all dimensions of life.

2.3. The Dichotomy of Control

One of the most notable doctrines within Stoic philosophy is the 'Dichotomy of Control.' Epictetus' famous distinction between what we can control and what we cannot forms the backbone of this idea. The Stoics urge us to focus our energy on things within our control – our actions, judgments, and reactions and to gracefully accept things beyond it.

The Stoic achievement of tranquility hinges greatly upon this understanding. By externalizing our locus of control, we saddle ourselves with needless anxieties. Acceptance of the uncontrollable liberates us, fostering inner peace.

2.4. Stoicism's View on Emotions

Contrary to popular belief, Stoicism doesn't advocate emotional suppression. Instead, it invites us to scrutinize our automatic interpretations of external events, which are often the root cause of our emotional disturbances. Rather than being 'passionless', Stoics aspire to attain a level-headed approach to life. Stoicism isn't about negating emotions – it's about refining them.

2.5. Stoicism: The Cosmic Perspective

Stoicism sees human beings as an integral part of a larger, rational order - the cosmos. Stoic cosmopolitanism implies a deep-seated respect for the universal human community. This perspective imbues an increased sense of unity with the universe, facilitating acceptance, understanding, and empathy.

2.6. Stoicism and Death

The Stoic contemplation of death is another cornerstone of its philosophy, promoting a life of urgency and purpose. Stoics advice us to 'memento mori' – remember that we will die. Such an acknowledgment is not meant to instill fear, but to awaken us to the impermanence of life, urging us to live fully.

2.7. Stoicism's Influence on Modern Times

Captivating the minds of people across myriad professions - therapists, entrepreneurs, athletes, and many more - Stoicism finds resonance with modern times. It has influenced everything from

Cognitive Behavioural Therapy to decision making in business and sports psychology.

In essence, Stoicism – with its focus on inner strength, endurance, and moral virtue – forms a powerful framework for human flourishing. Its timeless wisdom persuasively argues that happiness isn't found in external acquisitions, but within ourselves, in our approach to life, in the virtues we embody, and in the meaning we discover.

Immersing ourselves in the vast, profound ocean of Stoic philosophy, we not only perceive the world around us with newfound clarity but also comprehend the depth of our own potential. Stoicism helps us construct a fortified inner citadel to weather life's storms with grace, equanimity, and an unwavering spirit, thus drawing a compelling blueprint for happiness.

It's within this enigmatic, yet empowering, school of philosophy that the current exploration journey has its roots securely planted, preparing us to integrate this wisdom with the modern advancements of Positive Psychology in the subsequent sections.

Chapter 3. The Basics of Positive Psychology

Gazing into the realm of Positive Psychology, it is crucial to start by understanding its basic principles and tenets. Advocated by acclaimed psychologist Martin Seligman, this vibrant field of study leaps beyond the traditional focus on mental illness and shifts towards a more comprehensive approach to human experience, one that values an individual's strengths and virtues.

3.1. Unveiling Positive Psychology

Born in the dawn of the 21st century, Positive Psychology is regarded as a relatively new adjunct to the overarching subject of psychology. Its primary aim? To put the 'positive' back into the science, moving away from the pathological focus of traditional psychology, to concentrate on the conditions that contribute to optimal functioning, resilience, and richness of life.

Positive Psychology, at its core, is centered around the understanding that human beings want more than an endless cycle of symptom reduction—it is about an active pursuit of meaning, happiness, good relationships, and accomplishment. These serve as the backbone to the 'PERMA' model, a framework that outlines the fundamental elements of well-being: Positive Emotions, Engagement, Relationships, Meaning, and Accomplishments.

3.2. Positive Emotions

Positive emotions extend beyond the simple understanding of 'feeling good.' They include a broad range of constructive emotional states like joy, gratitude, serenity, interest, hope, pride, amusement, inspiration, awe, and love. Barbara Fredrickson's 'Broaden and Build' theory stands as a landmark in this part of Positive Psychology, indicating that experiencing positive emotions broadens human beings' thoughts and actions, therefore aiding them in building enduring personal resources.

Cultivating and entertaining positive emotions can have significant impacts on overall well-being. It triggers an upward spiral of continuing growth and thriving, as it enhances resilience and fosters the ability to bounce back from adversity.

3.3. Engagement

The second pillar of the PERMA model, Engagement, refers to the complete absorption in activities that challenge but do not overwhelm our skills. Mihaly Csikszentmihalyi's 'Flow' concept perfectly encapsulates this—flow being a state of 'enjoyment' or 'complete absorption' when an individual becomes one with the activity they perform.

Flow situations are those where a person's body or mind is stretched to its limits in a voluntary effort to attain something challenging and worthwhile. Such experiences promote skill development, increase self-efficacy, and contribute to a full, rich life.

3.4. Relationships

Within the social context, humans are inherently mutual creatures. Relationships, or more precisely, 'positive relationships,' form another integral part of this model. They extend beyond simple social connections and delve into the realms of mutual respect, love, care, and strong bonds of trust.

George Vaillant's 'Grant Study,' a 75-year longitudinal study on human happiness, emphasized love and relationships as a crucial predictor of happiness. This sentiment is captured in the age-old saying, 'Happiness is only real when shared.'

3.5. Meaning

The pursuit of meaning forms the crux of human existence. Many philosophical ideologies and psychological theories have reiterated the importance of meaning and purpose in life. Positive Psychology too champions the call for significance, marking it as a central element of fostering well-being.

Viktor Frankl's logotherapy, inspired by his experiences in Nazi concentration camps, is an excellent example of emphasizing the role of meaning in human lives. For Frankel, the primary motivation of an individual is to find meaning in life.

3.6. Accomplishments

Last but not least, Seligman's model draws attention to 'Accomplishment,' or 'Achievement,' as a key player in human well-being. This sphere focuses on having clear goals in life and the motivation to achieve them. Carol Dweck's 'Growth Mindset' concept, promoting the belief that abilities can be developed through dedication and hard work, perfectly aligns with this element of the PERMA model.

In the end, the field of Positive Psychology does not negate or undermine human suffering. Instead, it offers a more holistic perspective on human psychology, integrating the negatives and positives, the pains and joys. It equips us, not merely with theories and frameworks, but with valuable tools to lead a life marked by happiness, resilience, and well-being, bridging the gap between merely surviving and fully thriving.

Chapter 4. Historical Intersection: Stoicism Meets Psychology

The dawn of Stoicism emerged from an Athens stoa, the architectural framework standing as a symbol for a philosophy destined to withstand the test of time. Stoicism, harbored by intellectual figureheads such as Zeno, Seneca, and Marcus Aurelius, offers a pursuit of wisdom through the mental fortitude, personal discipline, and moral virtue. The Stoic sage aims to rewrite values and perspectives, vying for an unwavering endurance in response to life's enumerable vicissitudes.

Contrarily, the unveiling of Psychology traced its roots back to the 19th century, rapidly earning scientific recognition via the endeavors of Sigmund Freud, Carl Jung, and John Watson, piercing the landscape of neurology and the subconscious. More recently, the niche of Positive Psychology inscribed its mark under the spirited leadership of Martin Seligman, aiming to foster a fuller understanding of happiness and contentment.

4.1. Distantly Connected Philosophical Roots

Examining the roots of these two intellectual domains, it becomes apparent that while they originated centuries apart, a shared natal philosophy ties them together. The Socratic philosophical cradle gave rise to Stoicism, preaching the transcendental value of virtue, justice, wisdom, and self-control, unraveling a gateway to eudaimonia, a contented state of being or 'good spirit'.

Simultaneously, Socrates, along with Plato and Aristotle, imprinted a lasting impact on the development of western psychological thought. Their metaphysical investigations into the nature of the human soul and moral virtue laid a fundamental groundwork that inevitably underpins modern psychological theories, hence forming an inherent connection between Stoicism and Psychology at their roots.

4.2. The Stoic Reverence of Sound Mind

Stoicism prescribes a life guided by reason, advocating for an acceptance of fate while maintaining an intransigent spirit. Stoics teach that external events fall outside our control; instead, our effort should be focused on handling our responses - our will.

An integral part of stoic teaching underlies the belief that distress stems from erroneous judgments regarding the nature of events, rather than the events themselves. Sound judgments, aided by reason, serve as defense mechanisms against despair, lending power to the spirit regardless of the trials that life presents. This emphasis on mental proficiency directly resonates with Positive Psychology's accentuation of resilience, optimism, and personal growth.

4.3. Positive Psychology's Nod to Resilience and Well-being

Positive Psychology, rather than focusing solely on pathological aspects, seeks to understand and encourage the aspects of human life that make it worthwhile. It emphasises factors that enable individuals to flourish - what generates happiness, positivity, and a sense of life satisfaction? It also stresses the development of strengths and virtues to enhance individual and community well-being.

Resilience, a pivotal point in Positive Psychology, deals with the capacity to bounce back from adversity, stress, trauma, or tragedy. It aligns organically with Stoic principles, as Stoics hold that tranquillity of mind is achievable amidst life's turmoil through acceptance of uncontrollable factors and concentration on the amendable attitudes.

4.4. Stoicism and Positive Psychology: A Harmonious Symbiosis

Ironically, the ancient philosophy of Stoicism provides a baseline for individual well-being, while Positive Psychology provides empirical evidence to endorse Stoic assertions. Stoicism delineates a blueprint to obviate life's disturbances and enhance well-being, an objective shared by Positive Psychology.

Parallels stretch beyond conceptual similarities; practical techniques too find common ground. For instance, Stoicism's cognitive techniques mirror Cognitive Behavioral Therapy (CBT), a widely acclaimed psychological treatment method, reinforcing the strong interplay between Stoicism and Psychology.

4.5. The Continuing Rendezvous: Lessons for Today

The historical intersection of Stoicism and Psychology provides invaluable insights into individual well-being, resilience, and happiness. As our world buckles under strains from rapid technological disruption, environmental tumult, and geopolitical flux, these teachings carry a heightened significance.

Today's world could benefit greatly from a Stoic-style mental fortitude buffered by a Positive Psychological outlook. However, recognizing these philosophical and scientific ties is not enough. A renaissance of Stoic philosophy is required, in conjunction with a diligent endeavor into Positive Psychology, to accomplish a broader, more profound understanding of human resilience, mental well-being, and sustainable happiness.

Though initially perceived as disparate fields, Stoicism and Psychology intertwine gracefully to provide a comprehensive toolkit to maneuver life's jagged terrain, showing that though times may change, the quest for well-being and contentment remains eternal. Our pursuit of happiness, mediated through a unique blend of robust Stoic principles and vibrant Psychological practices, perseveres, bridging the historical and contemporary chasm while paving the way for a more resilient, content, and enduring civilization.

Chapter 5. Stoic Wisdom: A Guide to Everyday Living

A sense of tranquility radiates through the stoic philosophy. The purpose of life, according to the stoics, is to live in agreement with nature, which infers identifying and pursuing our most salient rational capacities. This philosophical school believes that the exercise of wisdom and virtue leads to a profound sense of fulfilled happiness. Translated to existing in the 21st century, weaving stoic principles into our daily actions can serve as a potent guide for everyday living.

5.1. Embrace the Dichotomy of Control

At the heart of Stoicism resides the idea of the dichotomy of control. Epictetus, one of the most influential stoic philosophers, argued that understanding what is within our control and what isn't is the core of an unfettered life.

Our internal realities, such as our judgments, desires, aversions, and emotional reactions to events, are under our control, whereas external occurrences, like the weather, the actions of others, or the inexorable passing of time, elude our command. Accepting this dichotomy equips us with increased resilience against life's challenges. It safeguards our tranquility, disconnecting our happiness from the unpredictable fluctuations of the external world.

5.2. Cultivate an Attitude of Gratitude

Stoicism encourages developing an attitude of gratitude. The practice of recognizing and actively appreciating the positive aspects of life nurtures our ability to stay content. It involves a perspective shift, focusing on abundance rather than scarcity, dwelling on positive experiences rather than brooding over negative ones. It can be as simple as acknowledging the warmth of the sun on your face, the support of a friend, or the opportunity to learn from a challenging situation.

5.3. Practise Premeditatio Malorum

A less intuitive yet systematically beneficial stoic technique is the practice of premeditatio malorum, or the premeditation of evils. This technique encourages envisioning potential negative scenarios or outcomes before they occur. Far from promoting pessimism, it serves as a psychological tool that reduces anxiety and increases preparedness by taking the sting out of future hardships.

Incorporating this practice within considerations of daily life—be it a challenging work project, a difficult conversation, or potential difficult events—can lessen the shock when faced with adversity, fortifying resilience and promoting adaptability and resourcefulness.

5.4. Embrace Amor Fati

Loving fate, or amor fati, is not just about accepting the circumstances we find ourselves in, but actively embracing them. Nietzsche, although not a stoic philosopher himself, notably championed this idea. It involves seeing everything that happens, however challenging or painful, as something to be welcomed, not avoided. It is a powerful mindset that transforms victims into empowered individuals, liberating them from the chains of regret and dread.

5.5. Maintain Memento Mori

In Latin, memento mori translates to 'remember that you will die.' Stoics utilize this contemplation not as a morbid fixation, but as a humbling, perspective-shifting reminder. Remembering the impermanence of life makes us appreciate the present moment more, trims away superficial concerns, and inspires us to live authentically, bravely, and conscientiously.

In conclusion, stoicism as a guide for everyday living encourages rationality, resilience, and acceptance. Combining these fundamental principles can positively influence our perception, response to life's challenges, and overall well-being. In this relentless pursuit of happiness, stoic wisdom is invaluable, offering clear, humble, and pragmatic guidelines for a fuller, richer human experience. It invites us to cultivate an untiring spirit, armed with the wisdom of what is truly important—virtue, integrity, and the capacity to greet life with serene acceptance, however it unfolds.

Chapter 6. Positive Psychology: Framework for Well-being

Positive psychology, in its essence, is an innovative field of psychology that seeks to study and promote the aspects of human life that make it worth living. Grounded in scientifically-backed theories, it encompasses elements such as joy, creativity, resilience, purpose, relationships, accomplishment, and more, creating a robust framework for overall well-being that transcends mere happiness or pleasure. This discipline, propagated by modern psychologists such as Martin Seligman and Mihaly Csikszentmihalyi, demonstrates a profound alignment with the ancient Stoic philosophies, which similarly advocated for a life rooted in virtue, inner peace, resilience, and acceptance.

6.1. Positive Emotions: The Foundation of Well-Being

Positive psychology posits that experiencing positive emotions is a fundamental pillar for nurturing psychological well-being. These emotions, which range from joy and gratitude to interest and love, are considered beneficial for both our mental and physical health. They foster an enhanced capacity to appreciate life's pleasures, build resilience against negative experiences, and establish enduring personal resources. Centuries before this concept was cemented, Stoicism upheld the practice of cherishing positive emotions, albeit wrapped in moderation and cognitive understanding.

Positive emotions are not merely transitory, fleeting responses to pleasing events. Through the Broaden-and-Build theory, Barbara Fredrickson, a prominent positive psychology researcher, posits that positive emotions broaden individuals' momentary thought-action repertoires, enabling them to discard habitual reactions in favor of more creative, flexible, and inclusive responses. This broadening effect subsequently builds various enduring personal resources over time, including physical, intellectual, psychological, and social assets that, in concert, contribute to enhanced life satisfaction.

6.2. Engagement: Losing Oneself in the Flow

The second pillar of positive psychology is engagement, conceptualized as the total absorption and immersion in activities that strongly resonate with one's core interests and strengths. This state of 'flow', a term coined by Csikszentmihalyi, is achieved when a person is so engrossed in an endeavor that they lose track of time and self-consciousness, creating an overwhelming sense of ease and contentment.

This notion bears striking resemblance to the Stoic principle of 'concentration', epitomizing the state where one is so engrossed in their duties that external distractions cease to affect them.

6.3. Relationships: Authentic Connections and Nurturing Bonds

The third pillar of positive psychology stresses the importance of relationships. Humans are inherently social, and authentic connections with others provide a foundation for psychological well-being. Positive relationships facilitate shared joy, provide support during hard times, and help people feel understood and valued.

This echoes the Stoic idea of cosmopolitanism, suggesting people are fundamentally interconnected, and bonds of mutual respect and understanding should be fostered.

6.4. Meaning: Life's Greater Purpose

Meaning, the fourth pillar, consists of belonging to and serving something beyond oneself. It is closely linked to leading a purpose-filled life. When an individual's life entails a greater purpose or sense of meaning, it elevates subjective well-being and nurtures resilience.

The Stoic philosophers also elaborated on the importance of purpose and meaning, reflected in their idea of 'prohairesis', defined as the commitment to life's higher principles and living in harmony with nature.

6.5. Accomplishment: Mastery and Achievement

Lastly, the framework of well-being in positive psychology emphasizes accomplishment. It is not merely about the success or mastery in external pursuits but a commitment to personal growth and self-improvement.

Stoic philosophy echoes this sentiment through 'arete', the pursuit of virtue for its own sake. It encourages the cultivation of personal strengths and virtues, proposing that true fulfillment and tranquility come from within, not from external achievements.

In conclusion, the sound correlation between the tenets of positive psychology and Stoic principles suggests a compelling unity, reinforcing the pursuit of sustainable well-being. Though separated by centuries, these two thought systems echo timeless wisdom, guiding individuals towards a deeper, more fulfilling understanding of life and happiness. Anchored in interconnectedness, resilience, meaning, moderation, and virtuous living, they offer a scientific and philosophical blueprint for thriving in our intricate, dynamic world.

Chapter 7. Resilience Building: Stoic Techniques for the Modern World

Resilience - the ability to bounce back from adversity and maintain one's equilibrium even under trying circumstances - is increasingly recognized as a critical ingredient for personal well-being. While today's psychology provides us with multiple insights into the development of resilience, we often overlook the ancient Stoic philosophers, who profoundly understood the importance of this attribute.

7.1. Stoic Philosophy: An Overview

Stoicism is a school of Hellenistic philosophy founded by Zeno of Citium in Athens in the early third century BC. The Stoics proposed that as we may not always have control over the events affecting us, we can always control what we decide about those events. So, for them, the backbone of an excellent and tranquil life is the development of self-control and fortitude as a means of overcoming destructive emotions.

7.2. The Intersection of Stoicism and Modern Psychology

Modern psychologists now empirically validate many Stoic ideas. Stoic exercises and cognitive-behavioral therapy (CBT), a prominent form of psychotherapy that treats problems and boosts happiness, share remarkable similarities. Just as the Stoics encouraged individuals to question their interpretation of events, CBT therapists propound that cognitive errors, or distorted thinking, can lead to unnecessary suffering. Both push the idea that changing our thoughts and interpretations of reality can completely alter our emotional states.

7.3. Stoicism's Approach to Resilience

The nurturing of resilience forms a central theme in Stoic philosophy. It encourages individuals to embrace adversity as opportunities for growth, emphasizing the development of resilience not just at the individual level, but also at a community level.

1. Mental Fortitude: The Stoics believed that our character and inner virtues are always within our control— not circumstances or material possessions. This perspective helps build mental toughness to overcome life's adversities, leading to enduring resilience.

2. The Dichotomy of Control: The Stoics taught about the 'dichotomy of control', holding that some things are within our control and others are not. Learning to discern between the two can help reduce stress and increase resilience.

3. The View from Above: This Stoic technique encourages a shift of individual perspective by visualizing the world from a broader, more disconnected point, providing a sense of peace and resilience in managing life's trials.

7.4. Stoic Techniques for Modern Resilience Building

1. **Stoic Journaling**: This involves writing about daily events, dissecting your reactions, and determining how you could have handled the situation better. It helps in self-reflection and the development of equanimity.

2. **Negative Visualization**: This technique involves contemplating the temporary nature of all things or imagining worst-case scenarios. Negative visualization can prepare us for adversity and lessen the impact of negative events.

3. **Meditation on Transience**: Stoics routinely practiced contemplating the ephemerality of life events, thus gaining improved acceptance and resilience.

7.5. Integrating Stoicism into Daily Life

The journey to Stoic resilience is not a leap but a series of steps, requiring consistency. Incorporating small Stoic practices into your daily routines can yield significantly improved resilience. Here are some simple ways:

1. Start each day with a Stoic quote, considering its application to your day ahead.

2. Plan for adversity by using negative visualization each morning.

3. Practice the dichotomy of control by acknowledging what is within your influence.

4. Make time for philosophical journaling each day, reflecting on emotional responses.

5. Conclude the day with a meditation on transience, fostering acceptance and resilience.

A blend of ancient wisdom from Stoic philosophy and modern psychological perspectives, backed by rigorous scientific research, can provide unparalleled resilience building strategies. Becoming Stoically resilient does not mean avoiding or suppressing emotional experiences. It means fully acknowledging and embracing these emotional experiences - but with self-awareness and understanding, we can navigate these experiences less destructively and more adaptively.

So, to plot a joyful voyage across the sea of life, it's incumbent upon each one of us to start developing the qualities of a Stoic philosopher. That's the route to heartfelt, enduring happiness which contributes to, as Aristotle put it beautifully, "life worth living."

Chapter 8. Mindful Living: The Stoic Method

The term 'mindful living' might be relatively new to many, but its essence is rooted deep within ancient Stoic philosophy. Rooted in ancient Greece, Stoicism exhorts us to exercise mindfulness, not just in specific scenarios or during isolated moments, but in the patterns of our everyday life. Let's venture deep into the Stoic method to awaken to our full potential of mindful living.

8.1. The Core of Stoic Mindfulness

An often-overlooked aspect of Stoicism is prosoche, the practice of attention. Stoic philosophers instruct us to focus on the present moment, acknowledging that everything else—it's either not up to us, or it's in the past or future, hence, outside our control.

Marcus Aurelius, the great Roman Emperor, said, "Every hour focus your mind attentively...on the performance of the task in hand, with dignity, human sympathy, benevolence and freedom..." By focusing one's attention on the task at hand, one can concentrate wholly on what's within one's control, fostering a peaceful mind while effectively addressing negativity.

Stoic mindfulness emphasizes the internal rather than the external. It advocates the cultivation of virtues, such as wisdom, courage, justice, and moderation, which are under our control. As one becomes more mindful of thoughts, actions, and feelings, the alignment with these virtues becomes more natural.

8.2. Incorporating Mindfulness in Daily Routine: The Stoic Way

Incorporating Stoic mindfulness in our daily life requires practice and can be done by following these key principles:

1. **Live in the Present:** Stoicism teaches us to focus on the current moment, discarding concerns about the past or anxiety about the future. For the Stoics, the present moment holds everything since it's the only thing within our control.

2. **Focus on What's in Your Control:** Discern carefully between what is in your control—your thoughts, actions, and reactions, and what is not—events, other people's actions or thoughts, the past, and the future.

3. **Maintain Equanimity:** Stay calm, composed, and unswayed by external circumstances. Realize the transient nature of all events and maintain your inner tranquility, a key virtue in Stoic philosophy.

4. **Practice Self-Discipline:** Through self-restraint and moderation, monitor and control your desires and impulses. This control leads to resilience, an essential feature of stoic mindfulness.

8.3. Stoic Exercises for Mindfulness

Stoic philosophers, like Seneca, Marcus Aurelius, and Epictetus, have all provided practices to help incorporate mindfulness into our daily lives. These exercises assist us to monitor and guide our thoughts and actions, promoting a fulfilling and contented existence.

1. **Stoic Journaling:** Stoic journaling can be a potent tool for reflection, allowing you to identify your behavioural patterns, emotions, and thoughts. Every night, review your actions. Was there any shirking of duties, perhaps rashness in speech, or lack

of self-control?

2. **Negative Visualization:** Stoics practice imagining what it would be like to lose the things they have. This is not a pessimistic rumination, but a tool to appreciate what one already has, thereby reducing the insatiable desire for more and the fear of potential losses.

3. **Stoic Meditation:** Stoic meditation is essentially a moment of introspection, where the self is viewed objectively. The idea is to detach oneself from personal biases and view the actions and emotions for what they are.

4. **View from Above:** A classic Stoic technique, the view from above, encourages us to visualize ourselves from a higher perspective, perhaps from the stars. This practice cultivates a cosmic perspective, inculcating humility, and an appreciation for the larger scheme of things.

8.4. Stoic Mindfulness: A Tool for Well-being

Today, more and more people are understanding the value of mindful living towards overall well-being. The connection between Stoicism, mindfulness, and positive psychology reveals a pathway towards cultivating a life of tranquility and contentment.

While Stoicism was not explicitly a philosophy of mindfulness, it has mindfulness at its core. By observing our thoughts, actions, and emotions, we can separate the external from the internal, develop an understanding of what is within our control, and foster resilience in face of adversity. It's important to remember that, as the Stoics advised, only through continuous practice can the ideal state be achieved. So, inculcate these principles and engage with the exercises that the Stoic philosophy endows. As we walk on this path, the purpose is not to eradicate emotions, but to rationalize and moderate them, leading to overall well-being.

The Stoic philosophy thus provides a holistic approach to life, embedding mindfulness in every aspect. By leaning on the wisdom of Stoicism, blended with practices from modern positive psychology, we can attune ourselves to a state of joyous contentment that emanates from within and extends beyond fleeting moments of happiness. In essence, living mindfully with Stoicism leads us to live with intention and perception, welcoming life with resilience, equanimity, and enduring happiness.

Chapter 9. Applying Positive Psychology: Into the Real World

Applying the principles and practices of Positive Psychology in the real world paves a realistic path leading us towards enhanced well-being and, ultimately, happiness. This pursuit is an exploration, an interactive journey, rather than a destination. The application is multifaceted, encompassing various arenas ranging from individual personal life to educational spheres, professional milieus, and societal dimensions. With the tools and strategies offered by this vibrant science, we empower ourselves to elevate our quality of life, boost our mental health, augment relationships and optimize our overall functioning.

9.1. Positive Psychology in Personal Life

At an individual level, the first step towards embracing the ideology of Positive Psychology is cultivating a mindful awareness of our emotions, thoughts, and behaviors. This state of consciousness is called metacognition. By recognizing, accepting, and understanding our internal experiences, we can disentangle from unconscious patterning and consciously choose our responses.

Emotional literacy is another key stepping-stone in the personal application of Positive Psychology. It entails identifying, understanding, and skillfully navigating our emotions. Affect labeling, or putting our feelings into words, aids in emotional regulation, thereby promoting psychological resilience.

Further, Positive Psychology teaches the value of harnessing our inherent strengths—acknowledging them, fostering them, and applying them in our pursuits. The notion of 'signature strengths' stems from positive psychology titan Martin Seligman and Christopher Peterson's classification outlining 24 character strengths that human beings possess. Identifying and leveraging these strengths not only ignite intrinsic motivation but also adorn our lives with a sense of purpose and fulfillment.

Lastly, the practice of gratitude consistently appears as a robust pillar in the study of Positive Psychology. Whether it be maintaining a gratitude journal or expressing appreciation towards others, gratitude practices prompt a shift in our perspective from what's lacking to what's enriching our life.

9.2. Positive Psychology in Education

Education serves as a fertile ground for the sowing and nurturing of Positive Psychology seeds. These principles can radically alter the school environment, bolster student development, and foster healthier learning experiences.

The promotion of social-emotional learning (SEL) aligns with the Positive Psychology framework. SEL is a process through which individuals understand and manage emotions, establish and maintain positive relationships, and make responsible decisions. Incorporating SEL programming in educational systems aid in improving student's emotional intelligence quotient, thereby cultivating a nourishing socio-emotional climate within classrooms.

Another critical aspect is teaching students about growth mindset, a concept presented by Carol Dweck, a renowned psychologist. A growth mindset, opposed to a fixed mindset, enables students to recognize their potential for development, viewing challenges as opportunities for learning rather than as threats.

9.3. Positive Psychology in Workplaces

Workplaces imbued with Positive Psychology values and practices morph into flourishing environments promoting employee engagement, productivity, well-being, and overall job satisfaction.

The introduction of a strength-based approach, as opposed to the traditional deficit-focused perspective in organizational settings, aids in enhancing workforce morale and efficiency. Employees who are allowed to perform in their areas of strength are reported to be more engaged and productive.

Also, fostering an environment of psychological safety where every member feels comfortable expressing their ideas and feedback uplifts camaraderie and innovation. This inclusion-centric approach engenders a cooperative and collaborative work culture.

Leaders practicing authentic leadership, a style promoting transparency, ethics, and positive role modeling, further enrich the positivity within the workspace. Authentic leaders inspire a sense of trust and loyalty among their teams, thereby contributing to the overall productivity and wellbeing of employees.

9.4. Positive Psychology in Society

At a broader scale, Positive Psychology harbors potential to transform societal fabric, influencing public policies, and promoting healthier community relationships.

Incorporating these principles into public health policies could shift the focus from disease treatment towards disease prevention and health promotion. Likewise, embedding Positive Psychology within social programs or policies can increase their efficacy by focusing on individuals' strengths rather than their shortcomings.

Overall, through its insightful principles and practical applications, Positive Psychology, when integrated into our personal lives, educational systems, workplaces, and societal structures, paves the way for multi-dimensional growth. It promotes a holistic approach to wellbeing, asserting that life is not merely about eliminating or surviving hardships, but thriving amidst them, finding joy in the journey, and harnessing our inherent strengths to flourish.

Chapter 10. Synthesis: Combining Stoic Philosophy and Positive Psychology

Stoicism, an ancient Greek philosophy, instructs us to embrace a virtue-based life, emphasizing resilience, tranquility, and equanimity, firmly believing that a person's chosen reaction to an event is in their control, rather than the event itself. Positive Psychology, a more modern approach to mental health, propounds fostering individual strengths and virtues to acknowledge and augment well-being, and thrive amidst life's challenges. The synthesis of these two powerful thought paradigms can become ground-breaking in our pursuit of enduring happiness.

10.1. The Paramount Principle of Virtue

Central to Stoicism is the belief that eudaimonia (a good spirit or divine natured state), or 'the good life,' is achieved through the practice of virtue, which encompasses the quadripartite cardinals of wisdom, courage, justice, and temperance. Simultaneously, Positive Psychology also emphasizes the significance of virtue, which is categorized into an elegant hexagon of wisdom, courage, humanity, justice, temperance, and transcendence. The commonalities amid these archaic and contemporary classifications propagate the immutable significance of virtue for achieving well-being throughout the centuries.

This overlap introduces an intriguing thought: can Stoic practices be successfully integrated into Positive Psychology interventions fostering virtues? An enlightening possibility that initiates this synthesis of ancient wisdom with modern science for enhanced well-being and happiness.

10.2. Handling Emotions: The Stoic Way

One of the most pivotal contributions of Stoicism lies in its perspective towards handling emotions. With a robust emphasis on emotional resilience, Stoicism celebrates the idea of 'apátheia' – freedom from destructive and disruptive passions. It encourages the practice of reframing perceptions and responses towards life's events, predominantly the negative ones. It propagates dispelling cognitive distortions and achieving emotional equilibrium through negative visualization, voluntary discomfort, and meditative reflection.

However, it is essential to debunk any misconception that Stoicism teaches emotional suppression. Instead, it endorses proactive management of emotions, fostering peace and tranquility. In aligning this with Positive Psychology, we see it echoing in the modern psychological approach of Cognitive-Behavioral Therapy (CBT). CBT, a positive psychological intervention, also emphasizes reframing cognitive distortions, demonstrating a remarkable intersection with the Stoic practice.

10.3. Positive Psychology: Using Strengths and Virtues

Positive Psychology, predominantly championed by Martin Seligman, is a robust approach towards mental health, shifting the focus from illness to wellness. It emphasizes fostering individual strengths and virtues, the factors that allow individuals, communities, and societies to thrive. In his 'PERMA' model, Seligman defined five elements that contribute to well-being: Positive emotion, Engagement,

Relationships, Meaning, and Accomplishment. This model can find a harmonic convergence with Stoic teachings in many fascinating ways.

The achievement of 'Positive Emotions' dovetails with Stoic teachings regarding emotional equilibrium. Stoic practices such as meditation, contemplation of the self, and dealing with adversity with equanimity can augment the 'Engagement' factor. Shaping virtuous 'Relationships' aligns with the Stoic principle of justice, emphasizing kindness and fairness. The pursuit of 'Meaning' connects with the Stoic end goal, eudaimonia, and the embracing of one's potential to contribute to the universe's larger order. 'Accomplishment,' which signifies flourishing in one's endeavors, mirrors the Stoic practice of self-discipline, perseverance, and commitment to duty.

10.4. Unifying The Two Paradigms

Stoic philosophy and Positive Psychology, while developed in contrasting epochs, share underlying common elements, enabling a seamless unification for fostering human flourishing. Integrating Stoic practices and insights into Positive Psychology interventions can potentiate their effectiveness in promoting virtues, strengths, resilience, and contentment.

The incorporation of Stoic meditation practices and thought exercises can enhance the Positive Psychology focus on mindfulness and cognitive-behavioral techniques. Stoic teachings on emotional equanimity can enrich Positive Psychology intervention aimed at nurturing resilience, emotional intelligence, and stress management. The synergy of these two powerful paradigms can unlock transformative potential, fostering an indomitable state of happiness, resilience, and well-being.

Thereby, combining the ageless wisdom of Stoicism with the bright insights of Positive Psychology can become a powerful tool in aiding humanity to cultivate resilience, equanimity, and enduring happiness. As Seneca, the Stoic philosopher expressed, "True happiness is to enjoy the present, without anxious dependence upon the future..." and this is where Positive Psychology comes into convergence with it by emphasizing the present moment's real-time engagement.

Thus, the sublime synthesis of Stoic philosophy and Positive Psychology can yield a comprehensive, robust, and effective approach towards the pursuit of genuine joy and lasting well-being. It's our vibrant voyage into the depth of human thriving, combining antiquity with modernity, wisdom with science. Now, isn't this an enlightening fusion to ponder upon and to practice?

Chapter 11. Toward Lasting Happiness: Stoicism and Positive Psychology in Practice

Few notions have captured the hearts and minds of philosophers, scientists, and the general public alike than the concept of happiness. How do we attain it? Can we sustain it? Answering these questions has involved not only reconceptualizing our understanding of happiness but also the ways in which we approach our own lives.

11.1. The Timeless Wisdom of Stoicism

The ancient philosophy of Stoicism dates back to the third century BC, with its roots in Athens, Greece. Stoics like Seneca, Epictetus, and Marcus Aurelius, posited a clear and concise framework for achieving a life of tranquility and contentment. At the heart of this philosophy is the doctrine of 'apatheia' – the serene acceptance of events without negative emotional responses.

Stoicism teaches that we can't control everything that happens around us, but we absolutely can control how we react. Thus, our path to happiness should involve focusing our energies not on changing the events around us, but instead on refining our perceptions and responses to those events.

11.2. The Modern Lens of Positive Psychology

Fast forward to the 20th Century, Martin Seligman - the founding father of Positive Psychology - echoed a similar sentiment. Seligman proposed a theory of well-being known as PERMA: Positive Emotion, Engagement, Relationships, Meaning, and Accomplishment. The aim of this theory is to lead individuals towards 'flourishing' – a state of lasting happiness.

Positive Psychology shifts the focus from traditional psychology's concentration on deficits, disorders, and diseases to aspects of life that make it worth living. Seligman posited that by nurturing these five areas, individuals can attain a high level of life satisfaction and well-being.

11.3. Bringing Stoicism and Positive Psychology Together

An exciting intersection exists when we compare the tenets of Positive Psychology with Stoic principles. Both approaches to thriving human existence converge on fundamental points, such as the necessity for meaningful engagement, understanding and managing emotions, fostering positive relationships, and recognizing individual potential.

11.4. Engaging with Life and its Challenges

Stoics argue that happiness stems from the proper appreciation of reality. If one can tolerate the imperfections of life with grace, it results in a peaceful outlook, ipso facto happier life. Similar to PERMA's principle of Engagement, Stoicism encourages an active relationship with the world rather than passivity or avoidance.

In Positive Psychology, engagement refers to the state of 'flow' - a state of deep enjoyment and absorption in activities that challenge us. Coincidentally, both philosophies value meaningful involvement, focusing on personal growth and profound experiences more than the fleeting pleasures offered by external events or material possessions.

11.5. Mastering Emotions for a Robust Life

Seligman emphasizes cultivating 'Positive Emotions' as an essential aspect of well-being. His view resonates with Stoicism, as both advocate for the mastery over our feelings than to be driven by them unconsciously. While Stoic 'apatheia' calls for objective awareness of our emotions, Positive Psychology encourages the intentional fostering of positive feelings.

11.6. Cultivating Harmonious Interactions

Both disciplines champion the importance of positive relationships. Stoics considered harmonious interactions with others as integral for a content life, much like Positive Psychology, which espouses the benefits of nurturing supportive relationships for good mental health.

11.7. Recognizing and Realizing Potential

Stoics believed in the idea that everyone has virtue within them, and living happily involves realizing this potential. Being virtuous, to them, meant achieving fulfillment. This mirrors Positive Psychology's 'Accomplishment' principle, which speaks to the importance of motivation and effort in achieving our ambitions and enhancing our perception of life satisfaction.

11.8. Practices for a Happy Life

While theory provides us with a framework, it is through practices that we can pragmatically summon happiness into our lives. Stoicism propounds several practices such as negative visualization, voluntary discomfort, and dichotomy of control, amongst others. Positive Psychology offers techniques like gratitude journaling, mindfulness, savoring positivity, and more.

These practices, rooted in both ancient wisdom and modern science, can serve as practical tools for anyone seeking to foster lasting happiness in their life.

11.9. Journeying to Lasting Happiness

In this thoughtful amalgamation of Stoicism and Positive Psychology, we unearth an inspiring pathway to contentment. By employing elements of both philosophies, we can attain a much fuller, satisfying enjoyment of life.

Happiness is within reach, waiting for each of us to discover it, embrace it, and make it a steadfast part of our existence. Interweaving the insights offered by Stoics and Positive Psychology can make this unforgettable journey to happiness a vivid reality in our lives.